Original title:
Celestial Circus

Copyright © 2025 Creative Arts Management OÜ
All rights reserved.

Author: Sebastian Whitmore
ISBN HARDBACK: 978-1-80567-862-5
ISBN PAPERBACK: 978-1-80567-983-7

Astrological Extravaganza

Jupiter juggles with rings so wide,
While Saturn's got hula hoops, no need to hide.
Mars rides a comet, a dazzling flight,
Venus sings ballads under the starlit night.

Uranus flips pancakes, upside-down treat,
Neptune moonwalks on waves to the beat.
A cosmic clown tosses meteor pies,
As laughter erupts in the darkened skies.

The Astronomer's Magic Show

Behold the magician in a starry disguise,
Pulling constellations right out of the skies.
Rabbits in top hats, but wait, they can fly!
At every great trick, the planets all sigh.

The telescope's spinning, a dazzling whir,
As comets do splits and the galaxies purr.
A dazzling performance, oh what a delight,
With winkles of stardust to brighten the night.

Celestial Charades

Can you decipher a dance from a star?
Pluto twirls round playing invisible guitar.
Mercury mimes messages lightning fast,
While the sun warms the laughter, a delightful blast.

Orion's a giant, mimicking plight,
And Venus just giggles, all covered in light.
The moon shimmers softly, a silent judge,
As games of the heavens make everyone budge.

Cosmic Dreams Beneath the Canopy

Under a blanket of shimmering night,
Galaxies gather for a whimsical fight.
Satellites swing, playing tag, oh what fun,
While little stars giggle, their mischief begun.

A comet trips over a wave of surprise,
While planets paint faces, with wild, silly eyes.
As laughter erupts from the stardust above,
Cosmic dreams swirled in a whirlpool of love.

Illuminated Menagerie

In a tent of twinkling stars,
Where clowns juggle moonlit bars,
Silly creatures leap and spin,
With every laughter, joy begins.

Jugglers toss comets with glee,
While unicorns sip cosmic tea,
The ringmaster, a wise old owl,
Calls for fun with a sly scowl.

The Imaginative Skies

Balloons shaped like wobbly fish,
Float with dreams and every wish,
Clouds form castles, bright and grand,
As giggles wander, hand in hand.

A merry band of starlit cats,
Purrs to the beat of twirling bats,
Frisbees made of shimmering light,
Chase the shadows in playful flight.

Enchanted Galaxy Gatherings

Dancing meteors swirl and sway,
As comets grooved in wild ballet,
Trapeze artists on beams of blue,
Flipping freely, just for you.

Fireflies spin in neon hats,
Bouncing high on laughter's mats,
The audience of planets cheer,
For every giggle echoes near.

Whispers of the Night Sky

In velvet darkness, shadows play,
With whispers swirling, hip hooray!
Shooting stars join in the fun,
Each twinkle wakes laughter, one by one.

A hungry moon chases the sun,
For candy flares, they start to run,
Galactic pranks and interstellar games,
Where joy is found, and no one blames.

Horizons of Imagination

A juggler with moons in his hands,
Tells tales of distant lands.
Stars tumble down like candy canes,
Laughter rings through cosmic planes.

Elephants dance on Saturn's rings,
Wearing hats and feathered wings.
Planets spin in a dizzy whirl,
As comets twirl in a joyful swirl.

Galactic Waltz

In the dark, a tango brews,
With stardust shoes and vibrant hues.
Twinkling stars move side to side,
As space itself begins to slide.

A chorus of planets sings along,
To the beat of a cosmic song.
Asteroids clap, a drum parade,
While meteors twirl in a grand charade.

Radiant Mystery

A magician pulls rabbits from the void,
Each one a planet, bright and toyed.
With a flick and a wink, they disappear,
While space giggles, oh-so-near.

Black holes puff their cheeks and pout,
Gravitational pull? They blurt out!
Fizzling stars in a popping show,
Wondering where did the light go.

Cosmic Mirth

Galaxies spin a web of cheer,
With whispers of joy that all can hear.
Space suits prance on a comet's tail,
As laughter echoes through the pale.

Shooting stars play peek-a-boo,
Silly wishes, bright and blue.
Gravity laughs, a ticklish friend,
In the arena where wonders blend.

Dancing on Solar Winds

Planets twirl in cosmic light,
Space whales dance in sheer delight.
Comets wink with a blazing tail,
While moons spin tales through the stellar veil.

Asteroids jive in a swirling line,
Shooting stars laugh, they feel just fine.
Gravity's a joke on this merry ride,
As rockets join in, no need to hide.

The Astro-Spectacle Unfolds

Galaxies giggle as they collide,
Cosmic clowns take the funfair ride.
Neptune's wearing a silly hat,
While Saturn's rings clap, imagine that!

Meteor showers, a disco ball,
Space-time bounces, we're having a ball.
Aliens juggling lunar cheese,
Giggles echo through the stellar breeze.

Lunar Puppetry and Starry Laughter

Little moons dance in puppet strings,
Pulling laughs from Jupiter's rings.
Stars are gigglers with twinkling eyes,
While Venus teases with clever sighs.

Cosmic marionettes float and sway,
In this frolicsome sky ballet.
With every laugh, the galaxies spin,
An uproar of joy beyond the din.

Enchanted Nighttime Performance

In the darkness, a skit takes flight,
Zany orbits in the quiet night.
Planets play tricks with comets' flair,
While stardust sprinkles everywhere.

The Milky Way giggles in delight,
At the chaos of the cosmic plight.
With every wink from the sun's bold rays,
We revel in this merry cosmic haze.

Moons Donning the Clown Shoes

Round moons in a jolly array,
Tumbling through night like it's play.
They trip on their own silvery beams,
Juggling the laughter and dreams.

With wobbly rings and comical traits,
They dance past Saturn's spinning plates.
Who knew the cosmos had such flair?
A comedy show in the air!

Cosmic Carnival of Wonders

Galaxies spin like colorful kites,
In a fairground, bursting with lights.
Planets bounce on a merry-go-round,
Singing silly tunes without sound.

Neptune's got tricks up his sleeve,
With a wink, he makes comets leave.
Mars spins cotton candy, oh so sweet,
While Jupiter serves up starry sweets.

Shooting Stars and Solstice Shows

Shooting stars dash, dive, and weave,
In a twilight show, one won't believe.
They slip on the clouds, burst into glee,
Painting laughs on the cosmic sea.

At solstice time, the planets parade,
In goofy hats, their charm displayed.
Starlit jugglers flinging bright dreams,
As stardust rains and laughter gleams.

The Constellation Spectacle

Stars in costumes, oh what a sight,
Dressed as heroes and jesters tonight.
Orion's got a fool's cap on his head,
While Ursa trots around, full of spread.

They frolic and dance, all in a row,
Creating laughter with each little glow.
With comets cackling, the heavens delight,
In this whimsical show, all hearts take flight.

Dancers in the Void

In the dark a jester prances,
Whirling like a star that glances.
With moonbeams wrapped around his waist,
He twirls and spins with all his haste.

A comet's tail is his grand cape,
He leaps through space in funny shape.
Galactic giggles fill the night,
As he starts his wobbly flight.

Orbiting Dreams

Around the sun, a clown will swing,
Balancing on a Saturn ring.
With silly jokes, he drops some pies,
While aliens roll their gleeful eyes.

In a nebula of cotton candy,
He juggles stars—a sight so dandy.
Sparkling laughter fills the air,
As he paints the cosmos with flair.

Chromatic Galaxy

In colorful hues the sky does dance,
As colors clash in a wacky prance.
A dragonfly in rainbow attire,
Zooms by with a laugh that never tires.

A truckload of giggles blasts through space,
With planets bouncing, keeping pace.
The universe is one big joke,
As meteors tumble, feeling woke.

A Night in the Cosmos

Tonight the stars wear silly hats,
As they float by with fancy spats.
Each twinkle's paired with a zippy scream,
Making the heavens burst with gleam.

A moonlit serenade begins to play,
With asteroids dancing in grand ballet.
Laughter echoes across the void,
As the universe's humor is enjoyed.

Celestial Revelations

In the sky, a juggler flies,
Catching comets with silly sighs.
A moonbeam swings from side to side,
While planets giggle, stars collide.

A ringmaster with a mustache bright,
Tells the stars to twirl in flight.
Saturn spins a wild dance,
As Mars attempts a romping prance.

Uranus wears a clown's big shoe,
While fiery meteors zoom right through.
Each starlet winks, a playful tease,
As suns do cartwheels in the breeze.

The jokes of space are quite a blast,
With laughter echoing, unsurpassed.
In this sky, both wild and free,
Adventures bloom for you and me.

Starlight Soirée

A gathering of twinkling lights,
With laughter echoing through the nights.
Jovial smiles from the morning star,
While meteors dance, oh so bizarre.

A party hat on Venus's head,
While Sirius shows off his tinsel thread.
Mercury's mischief adds to the cheer,
As comets toast with cosmic beer.

Neptune winks with a twinkling eye,
While Orion attempts to fly.
Each constellation has its say,
In this outrageous cabaret.

The evening ends with a cosmic kiss,
As galaxies swirl in splendid bliss.
Under the disco ball that's a bright,
Stars laugh and swirl through the night.

Astral Harmonies

A symphony of laughter in the skies,
Where shooting stars play peek-a-boo and rise.
Planets hum a merry tune,
While the sun yodels a daydream boon.

The galaxy sings with a cheeky flair,
A cosmic choir beyond compare.
Comets strum on harp-like tails,
As stardust swirls in playful trails.

Uplifting notes of cosmic cheer,
Echo through the void, crystal-clear.
Nebulas dance in colors rare,
As laughter paints the cosmic air.

The universe is tickled pink,
In this harmony, blink by blink.
As planets sway and stars align,
In playful antics, all divine.

Midnight Carnival of Stars

A fair of lights in the darkened sky,
With twinkling booths where stardust lie.
Galactic games and comet slides,
Under a canvas of shimmering tides.

The Ferris wheel is made of light,
Taking dreams on a dizzy flight.
With candy clouds and cosmic treats,
While black holes sing to rhythmic beats.

A ring of fireflies spin in dance,
As Saturn winks in a playful glance.
The bearded nebula tells a joke,
While stars burst out in joyous smoke.

With laughter echoing far and wide,
In this carnival, with stars as guides.
The universe giggles in endless glee,
In this midnight festivity, you and me.

Starry-Eyed Performers

Under twinkling lights, they prance and spin,
Juggling comets, with cheeky grins.
A moonlit tightrope held by a breeze,
Banana peels tossed, oh, such mischief, please!

Asteroids bouncing in grand acrobats,
Wearing bright tutus and silly hats.
Galactic laughter fills the air,
As space clowns honk, without a care.

The Universe's Grand Fête

In cosmic tents, where stardust flows,
Bright nebulae twirl in their fanciful throes.
A comet cakes adorned with sprinkles,
As the starry-headed jesters squeeze out crinkles.

Planets spin under a disco ball,
While black holes giggle, having a ball.
Zany lights twinkle, a glittering race,
As everyone dances in this wild space.

Starlit Revelry

An echo of laughter, a sparkly sight,
Space monkeys swing by, oh, what a night!
With nebulae strumming on cosmic guitars,
And meteors dancing, in swirling bizarre.

Shooting stars tumble, wearing confetti,
As spacefaring ducks waddle all set and ready.
The Milky Way sings a merry tune,
While alien balloons drift over the moon.

Cosmic Whirl

Galactic whirlwinds twirling around,
With merry aliens making such sound.
Hopping through space on bouncy rays,
With bubblegum planets in whimsical plays.

Bright stars spark laughs, they seem to say,
Join the fun in this far-out ballet!
A quirky brigade of Martian sprites,
Bringing joy to the whimsical nights!

Planets in the Spotlight

In a ring of stars, they come out to play,
Moons wobble and spin, oh what a display!
Jupiter jigs while Saturn twirls,
Mars steals the show with its dusty swirls.

Venus trips over her shimmering gown,
Pluto grins wide, but he's feeling let down.
Neptune's blues got the crowd in a swoon,
As comets crack jokes with a flash of the moon.

The Juggling Nebula

A starry juggler with arms made of light,
Tosses up planets, what a curious sight!
Galaxies giggle as they spin in the air,
While black holes laugh without any care.

Saturn's rings spin like plates on a stick,
While meteors zoom, making the crowd tick.
"Look at me now!" shouts a dwarf from his post,
And everyone cheers, for he's the proud host.

Dreamy Performers of the Universe

A sleepy black cat naps on a star's edge,
While galaxies stretch on a cosmic ledge.
A comet swoops down, with a tail full of dreams,
As laughter erupts in celestial beams.

The sun's a magician, pulling tricks with flair,
While asteroids giggle, floating in air.
"Now watch me disappear!" shouts a bold little sprite,
And space applause echoes through the night.

Astral High Wire Act

On a tightrope of stardust, a figure wobbles,
Balancing planets, and the audience gobbles.
With a wink and a grin, the tightrope star prances,
Falling in funny, upside-down dances.

Through meteor showers, the daring one leaps,
While Saturn's ring cheers in wobbly beeps.
Stars twinkle wildly, and there's much to behold,
As laughter and wonder in space unfold.

Aetherial Circus Act

Under the moon, the stars do waltz,
Juggling comets, without a fault.
Planets giggle, spinning round,
In this universe, laughter is found.

Nebulae toss their fluffy tails,
While meteorites dance on breezy gales.
Gravity plays tricks with balloons,
As stardust sparkles beneath the tunes.

Skyward Serenade

Laughter drifts on starlit air,
Shooting stars zoom without a care.
The sun and moon share a jest,
As clouds join in, feeling their best.

Galaxies swirl in cheeky moves,
While night owls hoot their groovy grooves.
Each twinkle is a wink, it seems,
A cosmic show, or so it beams.

Orbital Festival

Rings of Saturn wear their best hats,
Venus fiddles with cosmic bats.
The sun cracks jokes with playful flair,
While asteroids bounce with a cheeky air.

On this day, the cosmos unites,
Spectacles sparked in dazzling lights.
Orbits align for this grand spree,
As laughter echoes through the cosmic sea.

Chasing Celestial Trains

On a comet train, we all board,
With stardust snacks and laughs stored.
Chugging past during light-year runs,
Passengers giggle under shining suns.

The conductor's a friendly old star,
Bringing joy, no matter how far.
With planets peeking, full of glee,
Chasing trails of cosmic jubilee.

Galactic Fête

A clown on Jupiter does flip,
With stars as hats, they turn and skip.
Meteors dance, they twirl and sway,
While comets laugh and join the play.

A ring of Saturn joins the fun,
With laughter echoing, everyone.
Aliens munch on cosmic cake,
As Martians juggle while they bake.

Uranus starts a silly race,
While Pluto hides with a bright face.
Planets cheer, they shout with glee,
In this wild, starry jubilee.

Under lights made of shooting stars,
The whole wide universe is ours.
So grab a friend and come explore,
This fête of wonder, evermore!

A Galaxy Awaits

In a galaxy where laughter glows,
Planets spin in crazy rows.
A giant squid with a funny hat,
Twirls in space, oh just imagine that!

Asteroids toss some shiny pies,
While space-folk giggle, oh my, oh my!
A disco ball made of nebula dust,
Lights up the scene, it's a must!

A wild parade of alien pets,
Dance under starlight, no regrets.
Rockets zoom with a playful buzz,
As silly sunbeans melt with fuzz.

So come along, don't miss the chance,
To join the stars in a wacky dance.
In this vast expanse, laughter awaits,
In the realm where humor never abates!

Nebula's Enchanted Stage

Where starry lights twinkle and tease,
A stage unfolds with cosmic ease.
Galaxies swirl in a playful spin,
As funny faces start to grin.

A jester jumps from a swirling cloud,
Tickling stardust, bright and loud.
The moonbeams wrap around their feet,
Oh, what a sight, this dance is sweet!

With shooting stars as the audience,
An interstellar performance of nonsense.
The stars clap hands, a celestial cheer,
While funny sounds ring far and near.

Gravity's laughter pulls us tight,
As we spin and tumble, pure delight.
In this nebula, joy takes flight,
A magical show under the night!

Starlight Circus

Beneath the moon's bright, merry glow,
A circus formed in cosmic flow.
Jugglers toss the rings of light,
While orbiting birds sing of flight.

A bear in space boots does a stunt,
Making the crowd roar with a grunt.
Nebula wool coats bounce and hop,
In this funny realm, no one can stop!

A minotaur spins on a comet's end,
As laughter swirls, our hearts they mend.
Martian acrobats defy the odds,
With giggles and tricks, they beat the gods.

So join the fun, don't stand apart,
Embrace the joy, the twinkling heart.
This starlight circus gives us cheer,
In every giggle, we draw near!

Aetherial Jamboree

In the sky, the stars all twirl,
Planets dance and comets twirl.
Jolly giants wear big shoes,
While meteors play peek-a-boo.

Shooting stars throw confetti bright,
While asteroids juggle with delight.
Saturn's rings spin like a top,
As laughter echoes, never stop!

Galaxies join in, what a show!
Eclipses play hide and seek, you know.
With cosmic clowns in neon glow,
Smiles spread wide from row to row.

Twirling space dogs laugh and bark,
Rocket rides that light the dark.
In this fun where dreams take flight,
The universe shines, oh, what a sight!

Nebula's Serenade

In clouds of colors, they sway and hum,
Planets join in, oh, what a drum!
A waltz of waves with a silly twist,
As supernovas form a list.

Distant worlds play hide and seek,
With silly jokes that make you squeak.
Stars wearing hats parade with flair,
While cosmic rabbits jump in air.

Galactic giggles fill the night,
As moons make faces, quite a sight.
The starlight dances, full of zest,
In this universe, we're truly blessed!

Twinkling lights in a playful game,
Each one giggles, never the same.
A serenade from afar we hear,
In this cosmic choir, share the cheer!

Cosmic Carousel

Round and round the bright stars spin,
On a ride that makes you grin.
Galaxies whizz by with a smirk,
As the solar winds do work.

Nebulas swirl in a vibrant glow,
While moonbeams dance, putting on a show.
Silly rockets dart and dive,
In this joyful place, feel alive!

The orbits twist in a wacky line,
Comets giggle, looking fine.
Planets wave, don't be shy,
Join the fun, give it a try!

Mirth and magic spin like dust,
In this ride, we all must trust.
From dusk till dawn, let laughter reign,
In this carousel, joy's our gain!

Whimsical Heavens

Above the clouds, the fun begins,
Where starlight sprays, and giggles win.
With pinwheel stars that play and peek,
In the sky, it's joy we seek.

Silly sirens sing their song,
While time itself dances along.
In this realm of dreamers' delight,
Laughter echoes, shining bright.

The nimbus clouds toss fluffy dreams,
While comets join with gleeful beams.
Space confetti rains from above,
As planets shout, "Come join the love!"

With twinkling eyes and joyful hearts,
We savor every cosmic part.
These whimsical heavens, what a sight,
In this funny dance, we take flight!

Midnight Mirage

Under the stars, a jester flies,
With galaxies dancing, in bright disguise.
Planets play tag, in a cosmic swirl,
While shooting stars giggle, and twirl.

A comet bursts forth, in a burst of glee,
Eclipsing the moon, oh what a spree!
Nebulas laugh, in vibrant hues,
As they play hopscotch, on cosmic views.

Asteroids tumble, with a clumsy cheer,
While a chorus of starlings croak songs loud and clear.
The Milky Way grins, with its candy-like dust,
Creating a scene that inspires pure trust.

And as the night fades, fades with the fun,
The celestial jesters are never outdone.
In the vast night sky, silliness reigns,
Where joy is the heartbeat, and laughter remains.

Illuminated Wonders

Underneath the twilight, the giggles bloom,
Where meteors flicker, in a spark-filled room.
Stars play patty-cake, with silvered beams,
While the sun winks brightly, in daylight dreams.

The Saturn clown, in rings so wide,
Throws stardust confetti, with cosmic pride.
Jovian giants stomp, with thunderous roars,
Chasing down comets, behind candy doors.

Galactic jugglers toss planets and moons,
As laughter bubbles up, like helium balloons.
A nebula tickles a shy little star,
While black holes chuckle, saying "We're bizarre!"

From dusk until dawn, the fun never ends,
Where laughter connects, and joy transcends.
The universe winks, in a riotous play,
In this kaleidoscope night, let's dance and sway.

Colorful Quasars

A quasar beams brightly, in hues so wild,
Spinning tales of laughter, like a mischievous child.
Shooting stars waddle, with jellied feet,
While space-time giggles, in a rhythm so sweet.

Every twinkle a wink, from the vast unknown,
As the cosmos chuckles, it feels like home.
The universe sings, with such cosmic flair,
In this humorous dance, we float on air.

With cosmic clowns spinning, in whimsical loops,
While asteroids chuck popcorn, among starry groups.
Planets swirl by, with their silly caps on,
Inviting us all, to the Great Cosmic Dawn.

Where joy paints the skies, with laughter and light,
In this vibrant expanse, the world feels so right.
With every bright comet, predictions we make,
Is life just a joke, or a big birthday cake?

Rings of Joy

In the realm of stardust, beneath the glow,
Rings of laughter dance, putting on a show.
Orbits entwined with joy and delight,
While twinkling stars waltz into the night.

The sun throws a party, with rays so bold,
Inviting the moon, in a twinkling gold.
Each comet a punchline, that zips through the air,
As cosmic jesters spin, without a care.

Shooting spikes of giggles, from meteoric slides,
In the laughter of space, joy graciously bides.
The forever playground, up high in the sky,
Where tickling the void brings a happy sigh.

And as the night fades, the giggles persist,
A funny reminder, we can't resist.
In rings that keep spinning, joy's found, we see,
In this grand spectacle, we are wild and free.

Galaxies in the Big Top

In the dome of twinkling lights,
Planets juggle through the nights.
Stars laugh as they pirouette,
Who knew space could be this wet?

Asteroids tease with their wild spins,
While black holes laugh at all our sins.
Nebulas throw colored confetti,
As supernovas dance so petty.

A comet pops out with a cheer,
Winks at the crowd, then disappears.
With popcorn made of stardust bright,
Galaxies frolic, what a sight!

So bring your friends and take a seat,
In this show, the laughs are sweet.
Celestial wonders, funny and grand,
Join the fun in this starry land!

Starlit Acrobatics

Jupiter flips through the Milky Way,
Daringly swoops in a grand display.
The Moon holds its breath, a gasp from above,
As Saturn skips by, full of love.

Twinkling stars swing on silver threads,
Giggles erupt from their cosmic beds.
Meteor showers rain down sparks,
Sending Martians chasing larks.

Venus launches into a loop,
While Mercury dances with a goofy swoop.
Galactic cheers fill the dark blue,
As space-time squirts fun like a fountain, too!

With every spin and each wild twist,
In this circus, there's not a mist.
Join the stars in this acrobatic race,
Where laughter twirls in the endless space!

The Ringmaster of the Night Sky

In the vastness, a figure bold,
The ringmaster's tales of wonders told.
With a wink and a twirl, he commands the show,
As stars jump through hoops like a cosmic flow.

He cracks whips of light with a grin,
Planets pirouette, let the fun begin!
Each constellation in a jolly squawk,
As comets twist in a merry walk.

Uranus wears a clownish hat,
While Mars plays the drums, imagine that!
Laughter echoes from starry floors,
With each twinkling star, the joy soars.

Oh what a sight beneath the night,
A whimsical wonder, pure delight.
Join the laughter, don't be shy,
Under the gaze of the night sky!

Comets on a Tightrope

Comets walk a silver string high,
Balancing dreams under a starry sky.
They wobble and juggle bright cosmic pies,
Drawing giggles and wide-open eyes.

Stars cheer loudly, 'Look at that flair!'
While trailing dust gives a puff of air.
Galaxies clap with their twinkling hands,
Creating a ruckus across the lands.

Up and down, back and forth,
They spin like tops, oh what a worth!
With stardust confetti falling like snow,
The crowd erupts, "More, more, let it flow!"

So if you peer into the night wide,
You may find laughter, arms opened wide.
A funny ballet, so bright and bold,
Comets entertain with stories untold!

Veils of Stardust

In a world where comets tumble,
The planets dance and giggle, too,
A clown in a starry jumble,
Wearing shoes of cosmic blue.

Rocket ships play hide and seek,
The Moon's on stilts and doing tricks,
Jupiter's in a funny streak,
While Saturn spins with silly licks.

Galactic jesters flip and dive,
A sunbeam wiggles, laughs, and whirls,
Among the stars, they bounce alive,
With cotton candy made of pearls.

Laughter echoes through the void,
As starlings juggle flaming hues,
In this space where joy is plied,
Even black holes crack a ruse.

Luminal Gala

Balloons of light float in the sway,
As meteors cut through the night,
Whirling in this dazzling play,
Where gravity's lost all its might.

Aliens twirl in shiny shoes,
Spinning planets as they glide,
Stars raid the dance floor with their blues,
Jiving 'round in cosmic pride.

The Milky Way's a candy path,
Where cosmic laughter fills the air,
With every twinkle, silly math,
Numbers drawn in spiral flair.

At dusk, the galaxies unite,
To share their quirks and tricks anew,
As comets giggle under light,
In this realm where joy rings true.

Twilight's Improv

In twilight's haze, the scene unfolds,
A jester swings from crescent beams,
The stars will share the tales it holds,
As laughter squirts from cosmic seams.

Black holes wink with sneaky grins,
While asteroids rock the little stage,
Their antics spark whimsical spins,
Turning drab days to cosmic rage.

Celestial sprites on roller skates,
Zoom past the rings of Saturn's flair,
They pull off stunts that boggle fates,
Laughing loudly as the planets stare.

Underneath the twinkling glow,
This improv show never will cease,
With humor bright as comets flow,
In these night skies, bliss finds peace.

The Charmed Orbits

Through loops of joy, the orbits weave,
Silly satellites prance around,
With a wink and a giggle, they leave,
Eclipsing humor in playful sound.

Stars juggling asteroids with glee,
While rockets play tag with light,
A cosmic choir sings harmonies,
Bantering as they soar through night.

Planets wear hats, oh so grand,
With plumes made of stellar dust,
Their merry antics perfectly planned,
In this clamor, we can trust.

When dusk descends, laughter rings clear,
In the ringed ballet of space so bright,
A charmed world where all draw near,
In orbits crafted of pure delight.

Voyages of the Starry Sky

On comets we glide, with popcorn in hand,
Juggling the planets, isn't life grand?
Saturn's rings twirl like hula-hoops bright,
While Mars practices moves, a sight of delight.

The moon pulls the strings of a puppet on high,
Singing to Venus, a sweet lullaby.
Uranus chuckles, his jokes fly like kites,
As Neptunes form line for the cosmic delights.

Galactic balloons float, tied to a star,
With laughter around us, it's never too far.
Shooting stars fall, a shower of cheers,
In this circus of wonders, we'll conquer our fears.

So grab on to stardust and join in the fun,
The universe winks, the show has begun!
With laughter and joy, we'll dance 'neath the sky,
In this merry parade that swirls way up high.

The Ethereal Arena

Bouncing on stardust, a cosmic affair,
Where aliens tumble and float in the air.
Neptune's the referee, taking his seat,
While Martians juggle their sweet cosmic treats.

A ring of bright planets sparkles like gold,
Jovial jesters in costumes so bold.
With each little twirl, our giggles ignite,
As comets zoom past, what a fantastical sight!

In the stands, moonbeams are wearing their hats,
Sharing popcorn with silvery cats.
The sun shines its spotlight, all eyes on the show,
As galaxies sing in a whimsical flow.

We cheer for the orbits that whirl with delight,
As gravity dances and twirls us tonight.
With laughter and wonder, the crowd gives a roar,
In the arena of dreams, there's always much more.

Circus of the Stars

Twinkling tightrope walkers, balancing bright,
With shimmering ribbons that twirl in the night.
Jupiter's got clowns that tickle and tease,
While shooting stars race in a cosmic breeze.

The sun dons a hat made of sunbeams and spark,
As Mercury twirls like a dart through the dark.
Between the bold planets, the laughter erupts,
And whimsical critters join in with their jumps.

Galaxies whirl in a colorful spin,
The moon is the ringmaster, let the fun begin!
With each little giggle, new stories unfold,
Of wonders and mischief, all merry and bold.

So come for a ride on this comet so spry,
Join the wild antics that leap through the sky,
In this playful realm where the stars love to play,
We'll charm all the cosmos, in our own funny way.

The Milky Way's Marvelous Acts

Under the dome of twinkling lights,
Planets juggle in their flights.
Comets race with fiery tails,
While stardust snickers and exhales.

Nebulas swirl in a colorful dance,
Asteroids prance as if by chance.
Galaxies twist like circus clowns,
Winking at those in nearby towns.

Shooting stars throw pies in space,
While black holes hide in a tight embrace.
Rings of Saturn spin and twirl,
As moons giggle and give a whirl.

Cosmic laughter fills the night,
Meteors flash, what a sight!
In this show of endless fun,
The universe smiles, it's not yet done.

Orbiting Illusions

Round and round, they twist and twine,
Planets play a game divine.
Mars throws glitter, Saturn swirls,
A cosmic dance that twirls and twirls.

Venus winks with a silvery grin,
While Earth spins with a goofy spin.
The sun, a spotlight, shining bright,
While moons mime shadows, what a sight!

Asteroids toss around their hats,
While comets chase some playful rats.
In this orbiting grand charade,
Stars flash smiles that never fade.

Each orbit a jest, a merry-go-round,
Galactic giggles all around.
Who knew the sky could be so fun?
With cosmic laughter, the night is won.

Cosmic Fireworks and Fantasies

Fireworks burst in colors bold,
Galactic dreams, a story told.
Stars ignite with a crackling cheer,
As planets toast with a fizzy beer.

Pulsars blink like a disco ball,
While quasars twirl and proudly sprawl.
Shooting stars in a wild chase,
Sparkle and shimmer in endless space.

Flames of supernova light the void,
While laughter echoes, dreams are toyed.
Nebulas puff like cotton candy,
Cosmic circus, oh so dandy!

Each burst a giggle, a silly prank,
As stars form a giggling prank.
In this show of light and glee,
The universe dances, wild and free.

Gravity-Defying Stars

Stars bounce on celestial trampolines,
Veering from their cosmic routines.
Near and far, they leap and glide,
In this merry game of cosmic pride.

Planets somersault, giggling loud,
While asteroids dive, cutting through cloud.
With every flip, they cheer and jest,
In this weightless world, they're truly blessed.

Black holes hide, playing peekaboo,
As comets race, giving a view.
Wobbling orbs in an endless spree,
Twinkle and shimmer, oh so free.

So gaze upon this starlit show,
Where laughter and wonder constantly flow.
In this land of whimsical light,
Gravity's just a silly fright.

Starry Night Parade

In the sky where the giggles shine,
Stars dance in a line,
They twirl in their flouncy skirts,
While the Moon giggles and flirts.

A comet passes with a wink,
Leaving stardust in a pink,
Jupiter hops with a clownish cheer,
While Saturn spins in a ring, my dear.

Uranus chuckles in icy tones,
As asteroids tumble like rolling stones,
Neptune juggles with waves of glee,
In this fun cosmic jamboree!

The Milky Way's a playful path,
Where laughter blooms and never halts,
Join the parade, don't be shy,
Under the giggling cosmic sky!

The Zodiac's Delights

Aries springs with a bright, big laugh,
Taurus munches on twinkling daft,
Gemini flips with a twirling spin,
While Cancer wears a shell that grins.

Leo roars with a feline flair,
And Virgo shakes out cosmic hair,
Libra balances with giggly grace,
While Scorpio winks with a creepy face.

Sagittarius darts with a cheerful bow,
Capricorn nods, 'I'm all about the show!'
Aquarius pours out bubbly fun,
While Pisces dreams of a splashy run.

Under the stars, they stomp and cheer,
Each sign plays their part, oh dear!
In this rich tapestry of night,
Zodiac's comedy shines so bright!

Comet's Playful Dash

A comet zips with a cheeky grin,
Leaving trails as it spins,
With sprinkles of laughter in its wake,
It's a game of hide-and-seek, make no mistake!

Planets peek with curious eyes,
As the comet races through the skies,
Dodging asteroids, a merry game,
Each twist and turn is never the same.

"Catch me if you can!" it laughs aloud,
While stardust gathers in a fluffy cloud,
Galaxies chuckle as the comet plays,
In this playful dance that forever stays.

As the night twinkles and starts to fade,
The comet bows for its grand parade,
With a wink and a swirl, it flits away,
Leaving behind a night of ballet!

Planetary Balais

Round and round, the planets glide,
In a bouncing, cheeky tide,
Mars steps lightly with bright red flair,
While Venus twirls with cosmic care.

Earth joins in with a happy stomp,
As the Moon does a playful romp,
Pluto giggles, trying to stay small,
While Mercury zips, having a ball.

In this waltz of joy and jest,
Each celestial body does its best,
Jupiter spins with a booming laugh,
Join the fun, don't miss the half!

As they swirl and twirl on this stage,
Cosmic laughter is all the rage,
In the grandioso planetary dance,
Don't you dare miss this chance!

Whimsical Orbits and Cosmic Feats

In the sky, a comet jests,
Swirling round, a clown in vests.
Planets spin with rosy flair,
Twirling stars, a cosmic dare.

Jovial moons with giggles bright,
Dancing near the sun's warm light.
Asteroids toss candy bars,
Jumps and flips from funny stars.

Black holes grin, a swirling treat,
Where gravity turns up the heat.
Naughty nebulae play seek,
Giggles echo, cosmic cheek.

Galaxies chuckle in delight,
As meteors paint the night.
In this space of endless cheer,
Join the laughter, never fear.

Stardust Street Performers

Across the void, with tricks to show,
Starry jesters steal the glow.
Puppets made of fiery light,
Flip and twirl through the night.

Nebulas weave a magic thread,
While laughing comets bounce ahead.
Saturn's rings spin like a top,
As giggles never seem to stop.

A starfish juggles moons on high,
While asteroids join in the sky.
The big dipper sings a song,
As planets dance and laugh along.

Auroras wave their colors bold,
In this carnival of old.
With every twinkle, every glance,
We join their joyful, cosmic dance.

The Great Galactic Vaudeville

Underneath a twinkling dome,
The cosmos laughs, it feels like home.
Here, the stars perform their plays,
In whimsical and wild displays.

A cosmic cat juggles comets bright,
While a turtle takes off in flight.
Shooting stars do pratfalls galore,
Audience erupts with an uproar!

Planetary clown with giant shoes,
Slips and spills on the cosmic blues.
Astro-bikers zoom past with flair,
In this universe, none can compare.

With each laugh echoing wide,
Galactic wonders come alive.
It's a show, it's a game, it's a dream,
Underneath the starry beam.

Echoes of the Celestial Menagerie

In space, they frolic, bright and bold,
A menagerie, more than gold.
Planets prance on invisible strings,
While cosmic critters laugh and sing.

Shooting stars wear hats so tall,
In a ballet, they twist and fall.
Giggling plumes of dust and fluff,
In this zoo, there's never enough!

Time ticks on with a playful grin,
As galaxies swirl, thick and thin.
Neon comets race with flair,
While asteroids twirl without a care.

With echoes of laughter filling space,
Every corner, a new embrace.
Join the fun, don't hesitate,
In this odd world, we celebrate!

Celestial Cabaret

Under a moonlit tent, stars start to prance,
Comets in costumes, they twirl and they dance.
Jupiter juggles with rings on his arms,
While Saturn serenades with his swirling charms.

The planets all giggle, the asteroids cheer,
As they sip on stardust and nibble on sphere.
Mars cracks a joke, oh, what a delight,
While the sun plays the trumpet, so warm and so bright.

A nebula twirls in a dazzling dress,
Spinning in space, pure cosmic finesse.
With laughter and light, they share a grand toast,
To the quirkiest night that we treasure the most.

As dawn starts to beckon, the show must conclude,
With hugs from the cosmos and murmurs of brood.
But they'll be back next time, just wait and you'll see,
For the cosmic cabaret is the place to be!

Aurora's Dazzling Show

In the northern sky, a spectacle gleams,
With colors that dance like fantastical dreams.
The lights do a tango, reds, greens, and blues,
Whispering secrets to the night in sweet hues.

The sun peeks and giggles, quite pleased with the scene,
While clouds play marionettes, all fluffy and lean.
Each flicker and flutter, a playful embrace,
As the stars throw confetti all over the place.

A chorus of crickets plays music so light,
They chirp in delight, beneath the moonlight.
With every bright shimmer, the night comes alive,
In a vibrant parade where joy seems to thrive.

Then as brisk breezes dance, they begin to retreat,
Leaving echoes of laughter and warmth in the heat.
But fear not, dear friends, they'll return in a flash,
For the aurora's real magic is a colorful splash!

Celestial Ballet

In the depths of the void, there's a show on the rise,
With asteroids leaping through velvet-clad skies.
The planets wear tutus, all graceful and bold,
As they twirl in formation, their stories unfold.

Neptune takes center stage, draws gasps with his flair,
While Venus pirouettes, with elegance rare.
The meteor's quick steps, a sprinkle of light,
Turns the dark into sparkles, a true cosmic sight.

Galaxies shimmer in dazzling attire,
As the comets provide a bright, fiery choir.
With a clap of a nova, the audience roars,
For the artistry flows like a dream that soars.

As the curtain does fall, and the starlight recedes,
The dancers bow low, fulfilling their needs.
In the silence that follows, they hear the applause,
In the ballet of heavens, they took their own cause.

Beyond the Celestial Canvas

Painting the sky with laughter and cheer,
Drawn with a giggle, the stars reappear.
Brushes of light dip in cosmic delights,
Creating a masterpiece of whimsy-filled nights.

The moons wear a grin, all wobbly and round,
While the earthworms do flips upon soft, velvet ground.
Wishing stars tumble in a hilarious race,
Creating a circus of joy in their place.

The planets perform tricks, all silly and stout,
With Pluto as ringmaster, he'll never back out.
Through black hole loops, they glide with great glee,
In a canvas of chaos, the wild will be free.

And as the sun yawns, it's time to say bye,
With a wink and a nod, they fade from the sky.
But fret not, dear friends, for the fun will return,
In this glorious tapestry, we laugh and we learn!

Astral Fables

In the sky, a jester flies,
With twinkling stars and bright, wide eyes.
He juggles moons, both big and small,
As planets laugh and bounce the ball.

A comet's tail, a silly hat,
A giggling sun plays with a cat.
The Milky Way winks with delight,
As meteors dance through the night.

The wise old owl starts to croon,
A lullaby for the laughing moon.
Galaxies spin, they swirl and twirl,
In this grand show of cosmic whirl.

A shooting star trips on its beam,
And lands in a bright, cotton candy dream.
With echoes of laughter all around,
In the skies, joy is always found.

The Celestial Showcase

Planets parade in hats so grand,
With rings of sparkles, and bands at hand.
Saturn sings a tune from afar,
While Mars taps feet like a rockstar.

Venus does tricks on a silver kite,
With asteroids cheering through the night.
And comets swoosh, making a scene,
With giggles that echo from blue to green.

Uranus wears pants that are quite absurd,
While Jupiter rolls on with nary a word.
Neptune blows bubbles that float and gleam,
As stars all giggle, caught in the dream.

Each twinkling light a part of the show,
As they sing and dance in a cosmic glow.
With laughter and joy, the sky's a delight,
In the showcase of wonders, all shines bright.

Dreamy Comet Dance

Comets swing in a jazzy beat,
Painting the sky with rhythms sweet.
With tails like ribbons, they swirl and glide,
In a funny waltz, oh, what a ride!

Stars throw confetti, twinkling and bright,
As Saturn spins, capturing light.
A playful moon joins in the fun,
Shining down rays for everyone.

The cosmic crowd claps with delight,
As meteors shoot past, a wondrous sight.
Galaxies giggle, and the night's their stage,
As laughter echoes from page to page.

In limits unknown, they leap and prance,
In this jovial sky, they all take a chance.
Joy is the ticket for every star,
In the dance of the dreams, however far.

Echoes from the Cosmos

In the void, a riddle is told,
Of cosmic creatures brave and bold.
A quirky galaxy spins with glee,
Making faces at you and me.

A giant donut swirls in space,
Where black holes laugh, embracing the chase.
With starlight bubbles that pop and sing,
They dance around on vibrant wings.

Supernovae wear a silly grin,
Winning at hide-and-seek, they spin.
As echoes of humor bounce through the way,
The universe chuckles, come what may.

So, join the jesters, both bold and bright,
Embrace the echo of cosmic light.
In this grand tale, both strange and wide,
Laughter is the galaxy's joyful guide.

Tapestry of the Stars

In the night sky, clowns fly high,
With balloons made of stardust, oh my!
Juggling comets while laughing loud,
Each giggle wraps the cosmos in a shroud.

A ringmaster of dreams spins tales untold,
Whispering secrets of galaxies bold.
Planets strut in mismatched shoes,
Dancing to rhythms that they all choose.

Nebulas chuckle, swirling in glee,
As meteors race, setting wishes free.
Stars play tag in the velvet night,
While moonbeams bounce with delight, oh what a sight!

So come take a seat in this wacky night,
Where stars wear hats, and the sky is bright.
Join the laughter that's endless and clear,
In this grand show, there's nothing to fear.

Choreography of Light

Twinkling lanterns twirl in the dark,
Shooting lasers play, leaving their mark.
The disco sun spins on its axis with flair,
While planets shimmy without a care.

A ballet of beams, a pirouette of rays,
Galactic dancers in a starry ballet.
Nebulas leap in a colorful spree,
While black holes laugh at the way things can be.

Comets tap dance, with tails flowing wide,
Each shimmer and glimmer, a joyous ride.
Light-years of laughter echo through space,
In this grand performance, we all find our place.

So grab your popcorn, it's showtime tonight,
As shadows and starlight join in delight.
With giggles that ripple through all we behold,
This cosmic cabaret never gets old.

Celestial Whims

In galaxies far, where the oddballs reside,
Black holes juggle while asteroids slide.
Puppies made of stardust bark from afar,
As zebras on comets play twinkle guitar.

A sunbeam slips in on a banana peel,
While the moon spins tales that make us all squeal.
Stars wear pajamas to giggle all night,
In pajamas adorned with bright comical light.

The silly stars wink, with mischief in tow,
As giggling galaxies put on their show.
With inverted rainbows and candy cane skies,
The universe glimmers with playful surprise.

So come one, come all, to this whimsical scene,
Where the odd is the norm, and life's just a dream.
In a cosmic abode where laughter takes flight,
Join in the fun of this dazzling night.

The Universe's Theater

The curtain of night rises with cheer,
Watch as the stars pull each other near.
A comedian comet takes center stage,
Cracking up black holes, making them rage.

Planets applaud with their eccentric orbits,
While supernovae flash their bright sprints.
The galaxy hums in a silly jig,
As Saturn's rings dance with a playful wig.

The audience gasps as quarks take the mic,
Slinging their jokes with quick cosmic strike.
Laughter erupts, echoing wide,
In this theater of wonders, no need to hide.

So step into the cosmos, the laughter's your guide,
With each shooting star, we're all filled with pride.
In this whimsical play where joy takes its turn,
The universe spins, and we all brightly yearn.

Ethereal Encounters

In the night sky, clowns take flight,
With shiny balloons and twinkling light.
Juggling stars while riding comets,
They tickle the moon, oh what a sonnet!

A lion roars made of shooting stars,
He plays the piano on Jupiter's bars.
Martians tap dance in goofy shoes,
While a comet sweeps in, with cosmic blues!

Giggles echo from alien crowds,
Flying discs form whimsical shrouds.
Popcorn made of stardust rains,
And everyone cheers, forgetting their pains.

They somersault beneath Saturn's rings,
While space kittens dance and sing.
Laughter ripples through the stellar night,
Ethereal encounters, what pure delight!

Shadows of the Milky Way

In the shadows of stars, a jest unfolds,
With cosmic tricksters, laughter foretold.
A giraffe in a rocket, soaring so high,
Peeking at planets, that curious guy!

Celestial mimes, with silent routines,
Spinning tales woven in moonbeam seams.
The saturnine ringmaster shouts and prances,
As quirky meteors join for their dances.

Witty whispers of quasars gleam,
A magic show conjuring space dust dream.
Aliens in tutus make a silly scene,
While comets chase dreams on a cosmic screen.

Constellations giggle, their laughter so bright,
As they juggle the planets with pure delight.
In shadows of night where stardust can sway,
The funny parade twirls in a sparkling way!

Twinkling Whimsy

A puppy spins in zero-gravity,
While smiling planets cheer with glee.
Jovial giants throw a glitter spree,
As they dance with stars, oh so carefree!

Space owls hoot their chorus of fun,
While asteroids race beneath the sun.
The nebula blooms in colorful flair,
Laughter and joy float in the air.

Tiny fairies in bright costumes glow,
Eating candy made of meteor snow.
Wobbling robots add to the thrill,
With comical dances and jazzy skill.

In this vibrant tapestry spun bright,
Whimsy awakens in the heart of night.
As twinkling sprites leap from star to star,
The universe chuckles, it's ended so far!

Stellar Festival of Lights

A carnival blooms on a distant sphere,
Bright lights twinkle, bringing such cheer.
Rocket rides twist and twirl with delight,
While neon creatures splash through the night.

Shooting stars whiz by with a wink,
Acrobatic aliens carefully think.
Luminous poodles prance and parade,
Under moonlit tents, happiness made.

Fluffy clouds form sweet cotton candy,
The laughter of comets, oh so dandy.
Flip-flopping foxes play leapfrog,
As solar flares dance, with a lightning smog!

In all this splendor, the universe beams,
Funny oddities float through our dreams.
A festival where everything's right,
Celebrating creation in blissful light!

The Great Cosmic Showdown

In the ring of stars they prance,
A comet's dance, a moonlit chance,
With asteroids hurling pies and cakes,
And laughter echoes, no room for fakes.

Planets juggle, what a sight,
Saturn spins, with all its might,
While goofy aliens throw confetti,
As space cows graze, all warm and sweaty.

Nebula clowns with colors bright,
Tickle the sun with sheer delight,
They tumble through bright solar flares,
No worries here, just cosmic airs.

A black hole swallows the final show,
With friends all sharing the cosmic glow,
In this vast expanse, joy abounds,
In the quirkiest dance among the sounds.

Stardust Masque

Under twinkling gems on high,
Masks of starlight, oh my, oh my,
Jovian ladies wear gowns of glow,
While Martian gents put on quite the show.

Comets dash in diaphanous veils,
While Milky Way provides the trails,
Cosmic popcorn raining down,
As Venus spins in her silly gown.

A jester floats on cosmic seas,
Tickling planets with a breeze,
The giggles ripple through the void,
As darker matters are enjoyed.

A party like no other seen,
In this interstellar dream machine,
With laughter ringing through the arcs,
The universe shines with colorful sparks.

Harmonies of the Heavens

Listen close, the stars compose,
A symphony that ebbs and glows,
Wobbling planets hum off-key,
Causing chuckles in the spree.

Asteroids bang with clumsy glee,
Singing tunes from A to Z,
Galactic choirs, full of cheer,
Echo through the universe here.

Meteor showers strum the strings,
As solar flares do funny swings,
With every note, a wink, a wink,
In this vastness, the universe thinks.

Dance of the comets, oh so spry,
With twinkling laughter in the sky,
Wrapping the cosmos in a hug,
Jovial rhythms, like a friendly bug.

Constellation's Charm

In the tapestry of night they play,
With starry giggles, come what may,
The Big Dipper spills its drink,
As the little stars begin to wink.

Orion's belt slips down its waist,
While Ursa Major picks up the pace,
A dance of light, a glittering crew,
With playful suns winking at you.

The silly stars with laughter fly,
Swirling 'round in a cosmic pie,
A sprinkle of fun in every glance,
The universe throws a joyous dance.

When morning comes, the jokes persist,
As shadows fade, they can't resist,
Though hidden now, they plot and scheme,
For night will come, back to the dream.

Dance of the Constellations

Up in the sky, stars jump high,
Galaxies swirl in the night sky.
Laughter echoes through the dark,
Planets prance like they're at a lark.

Comets zoom, tails all ablaze,
Moonbeams twinkle in a silly daze.
Saturn spins in a hula-hoop,
While Jupiter leads a starry troop.

Uranus winks, doing a twist,
Stars declare, 'You can't resist!'
Planets frolic with bells that chime,
As they groove to the music of time.

Galactic giggles fill the void,
Celestial beings, they can't avoid.
Each twirl and spin brings delight,
In this cosmic, kaleidoscopic night.

Twinkling Carnival

At dusk, the sky's a vibrant fair,
Where fireflies dance without a care.
Nebulae glow like cotton candy,
Bright meteors shoot, oh so dandy!

Stars wear hats, and moons in ties,
A comet's dance, a sweet surprise.
With popcorn clouds, the giants munch,
While asteroids gather for a crunch.

Rings around planets spin with glee,
Galactic music floats like a bee.
Venus flips like a juggling star,
Springing high with a giggling car.

So join the fun, grab a space seat,
As laughter rings from the astral fleet.
A banquet of joy in a boundless dome,
Where every star is free to roam.

Celestial Menagerie

Behold the zoo of starry sights,
Where comets play and rocket fights.
A bear made of stardust grins wide,
As meteors race on a merry ride.

Galactic goats hop from star to star,
While fish made of light swim afar.
A lion with a constellation mane,
Roars in laughter, embracing the game.

Zany zebras, in stripes of light,
Run through the night, what a funny sight!
Elephants dance with glittering sighs,
As the universe bursts into cries.

Join the fun in this cosmic play,
Where every creature finds its way.
In this menagerie of astral cheer,
Stars and laughter fill every sphere.

Astral Masquerade

Beneath the stars, a grand parade,
Where every planet wears a trade.
Dressed in ribbons of glowing light,
Each orbits on this festive night.

Venus dons a sparkling gown,
While Mars slides by with a twirling crown.
Neptune juggles with a playful hook,
Uranus strikes a regal look.

A swirling mist, the Milky Way,
Holds secrets of this stellar play.
Constellations laugh and wink,
As starry spirits dance and drink.

Jupiter leads in a comical jig,
With Saturn spinning, oh so big.
Galaxies spin, the night shines bright,
In this dance of the cosmic light.

www.ingramcontent.com/pod-product-compliance
Lightning Source LLC
Chambersburg PA
CBHW051654160426
43209CB00004B/895